D1809352

TECHNICAL REQUIREMENTS FOR PIANO

WITH EXERCISES IN EAR TRAINING AND SIGHT READING

Book 3

Compiled and edited by Boris Berlin and Clifford Poole

Revised in accordance with the Grade 3 examination requirements of the
Royal Conservatory of Music

ISBN 0-88797-157-1

© Copyright 1984 The Frederick Harris Music Co., Limited
Oakville, Ontario, Canada

Printed in Canada

"It goes without saying that technical proficiency should be one of the first acquisitions of the student who would become a fine pianist."

— SERGEI RACHMANINOFF

CONTENTS

Examination Material

Optional Material

SCALES

Keys of F, B flat, and A major; A, D, and G minor, Harmonic and Melodic.
Hands separately, two octaves, ascending and descending, in eighth notes.
M.M. ♩ = 92 (Minimum speed)

6th or 7th note raised 1/2 a tone & lowered on the way down

A minor, Melodic

D minor, Harmonic

D minor, Melodic

G minor, Harmonic

G minor, Melodic

FORMULA PATTERN SCALE

Key of C major , G+
Hands together, in eighth notes.
Moderate tempo.

C major, Formula pattern

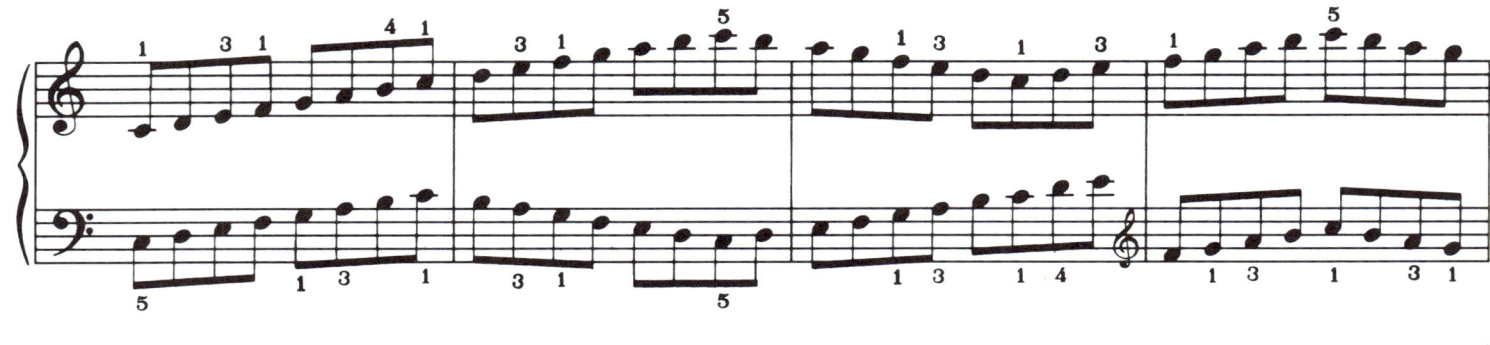

TRIADS

Keys of F, B flat, and A major, A, D, and G minor.
Root position and inversions, ascending and descending.
Hands separately, one octave.

Solid form in quarter notes, M.M. ♩ = 132 (Minimum speed)

Broken form in triplet eighth notes, M.M. ♩ = 72 (Minimum speed)

Solid
Right Hand 3 times a day

F major

Broken
Right Hand

Left Hand

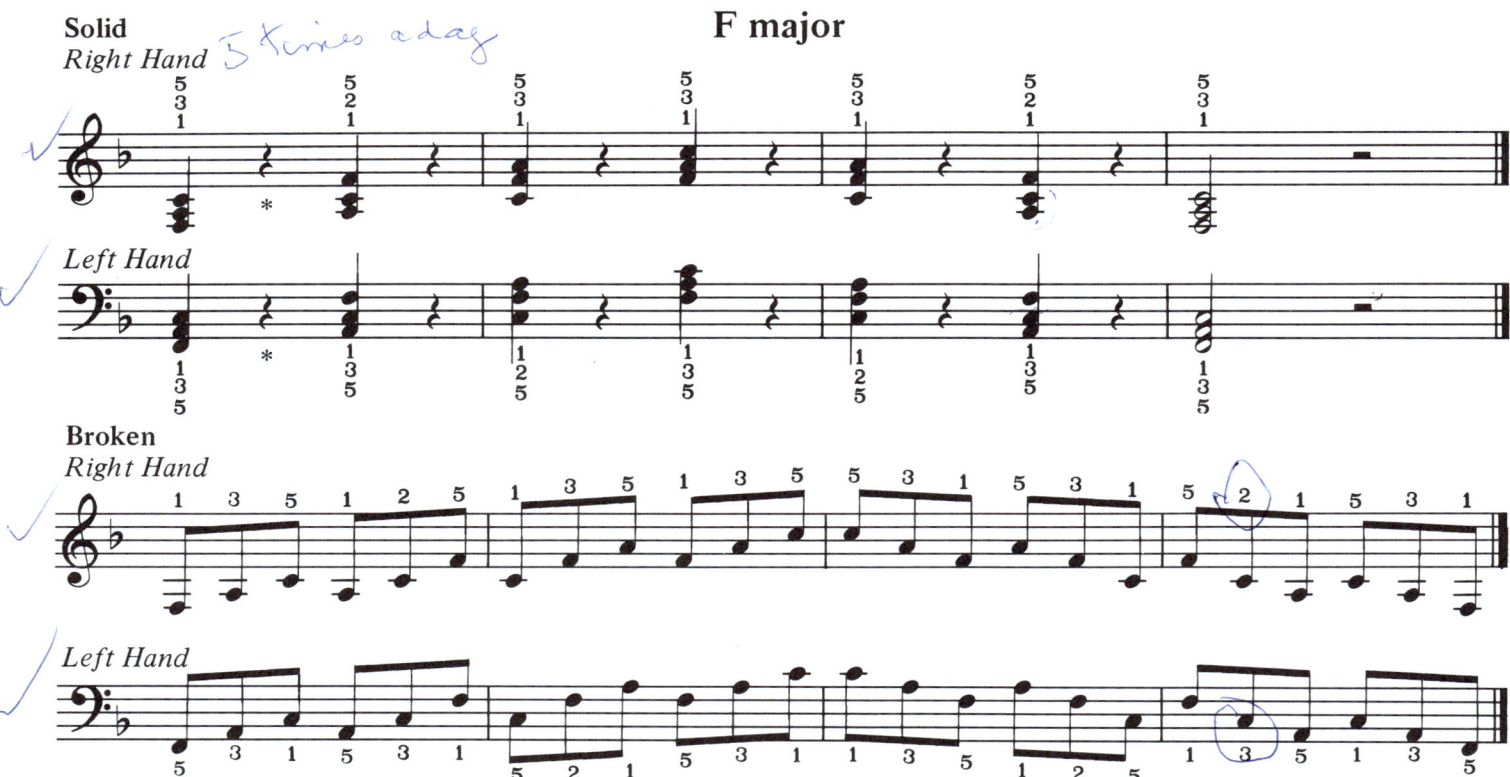

*Use the rests to prepare the following chord.

B flat major

A major

A minor

8

Broken
Right Hand

Left Hand

D minor

Solid
Right Hand

Left Hand

Broken
Right Hand

Left Hand

G minor

Solid
Right Hand

Left Hand

Broken
Right Hand

Left Hand

EAR TEST EXERCISES

1. The teacher or parent plays a short melody twice in two-four or three-four time, as in the examples shown below. (The student must not look at the music.)

The student then imitates the rhythmic pattern of the melody by singing, clapping, or tapping it from memory.

The student may practise by singing, clapping, or tapping the rhythmic patterns of the examples shown below and of other tunes the teacher or parent plays.

2. The teacher or parent names a key (C, G, F, or D major), plays the tonic triad, then plays a melody of 5 notes twice. The melody will begin on the tonic or mediant, and will be based on the first 5 notes of the scale, as in the examples shown below. The melody may contain a skip of a third and/or a skip of a fifth. (The student must see neither the music nor the keyboard.)

The student must play back the same melody from memory.

The student may practise by playing the following melodies, then singing them from memory in correct time and pitch to the syllable "lah", or to 1 (Do), 2 (Ré), 3 (Mi).

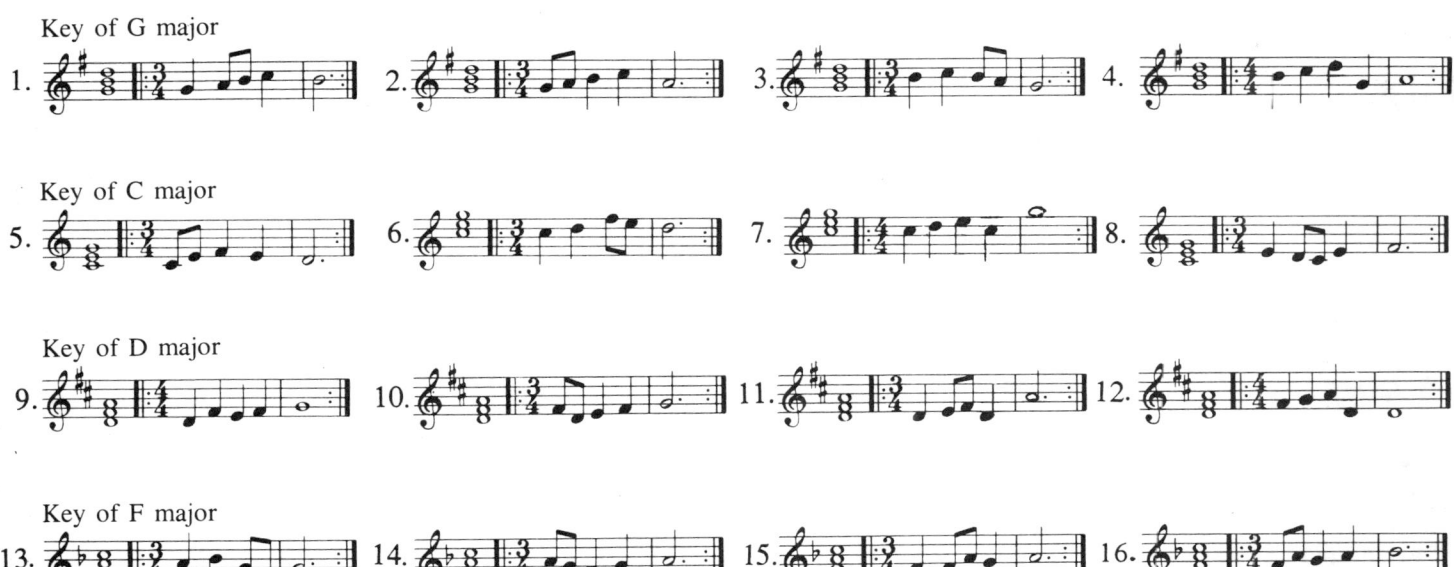

3. The teacher or parent plays a note and the student then sings or hums any of the intervals shown below; OR

The teacher or parent plays an interval in broken form, as in the examples shown below, and the student identifies the interval by ear. (The student must see neither the music nor the keyboard.)

The student may practise by singing the following intervals after striking the first note, then playing the second note to test accuracy. The register of any of the intervals may be changed to suit the range of the student's voice.

(above a given note)

Major third

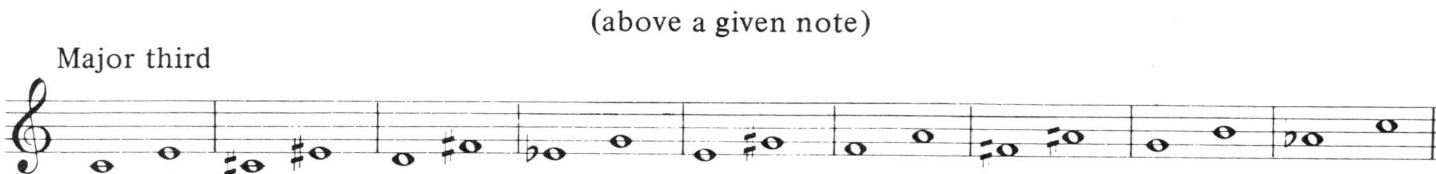

Perfect fifth

Perfect octave

(below a given note)

Minor third

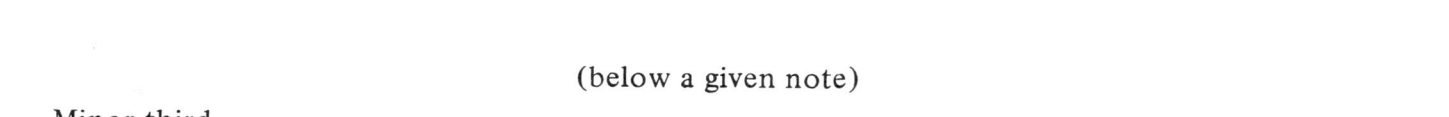

Perfect fifth

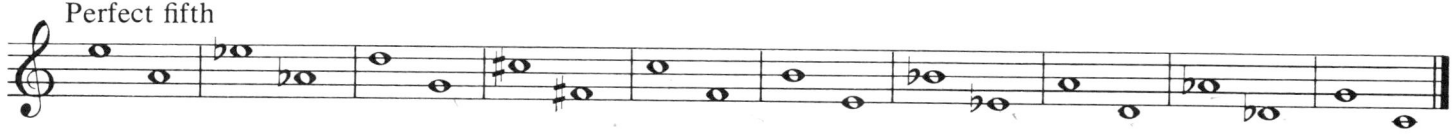

Additional exercises may be found on page 16.

EXERCISES IN SIGHT READING

Although it is not required for the examination, the student is strongly advised to practise counting out loud.

No. 8

No. 9

Clap or tap this rhythmic pattern.

No. 10

No. 11

Clap or tap this rhythmic pattern.

No. 12

No. 13

Clap or tap this rhythmic pattern.

No. 14

FUN PIECES

These little pieces have problems beyond the Grade 3 sight reading level.
They can be used for "quick study" as well as for sight reading.
Enjoy them!

Pensive

Clifford Poole

Easter

Clifford Poole

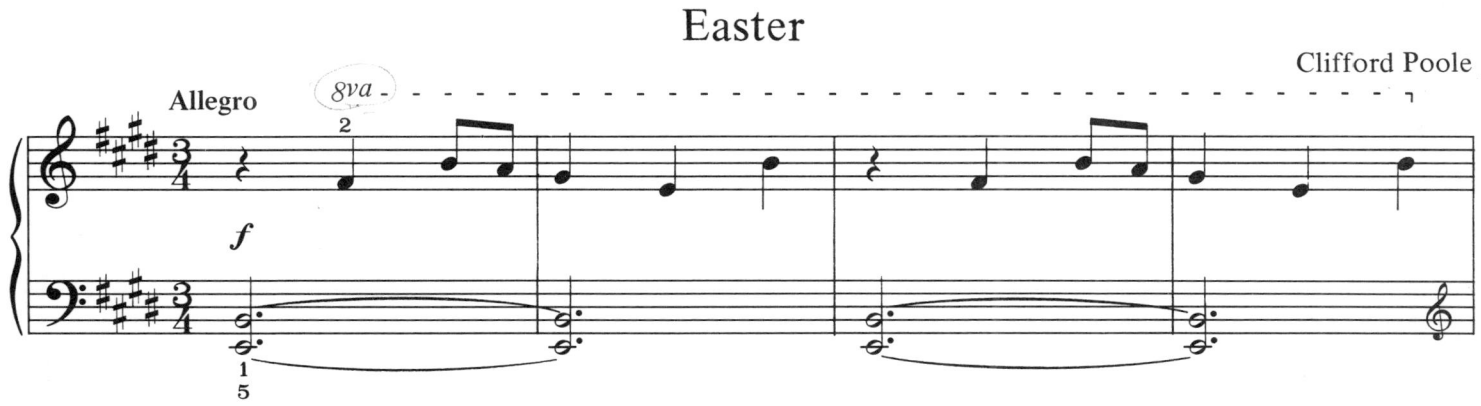

Depress the right pedal with the right foot and hold throughout the piece.

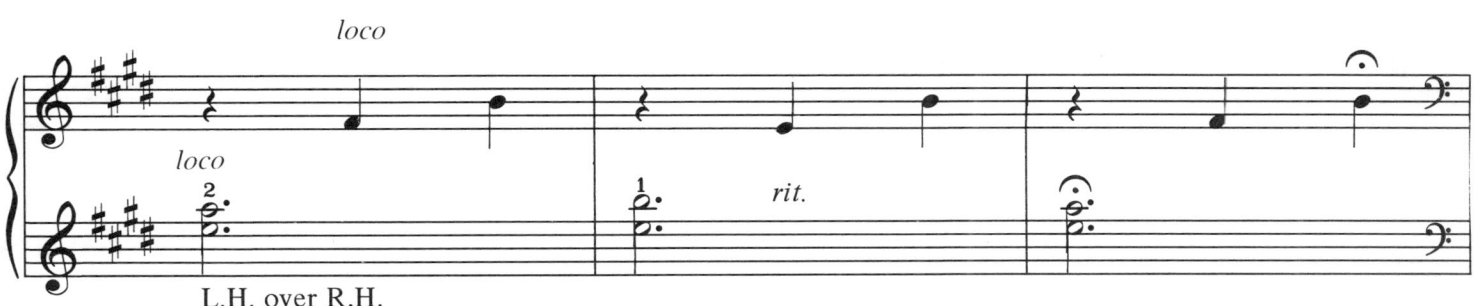

L.H. over R.H.

March

Allegro

Clifford Poole

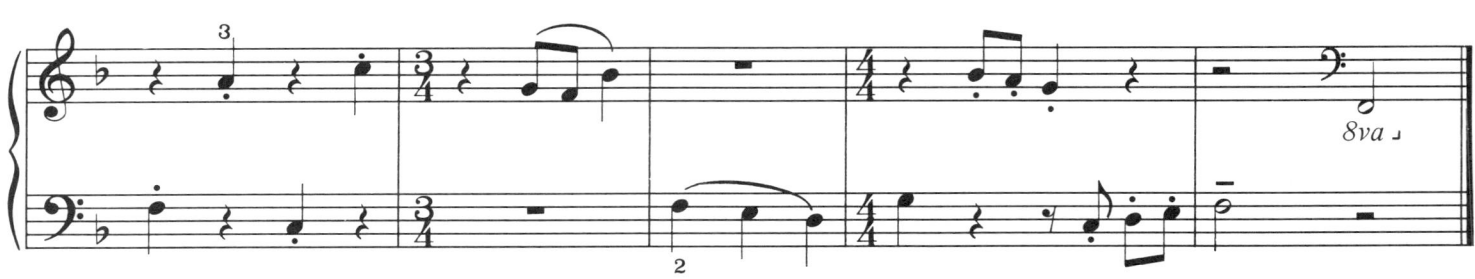

The Little Mexican Boy

Allegretto

Clifford Poole

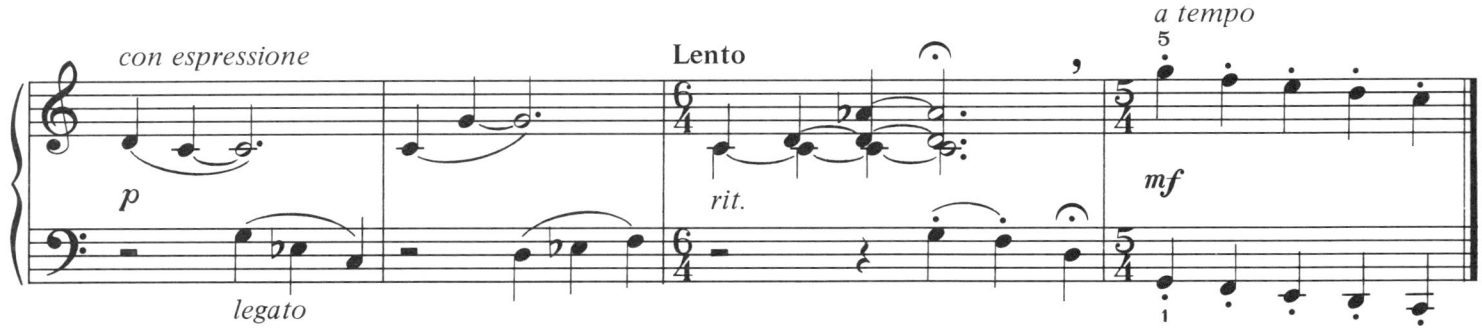

SCALE EXERCISES

These exercises, although not required for the examination, will, if practised carefully and diligently, help the student acquire the ability to play technical tests evenly, with good tone, and with logical fingering.

Although these exercises are in C major, they should be practised hands separately in all the required keys using normal thumb positions. The exercises may also be practised hands together.

C. Poole

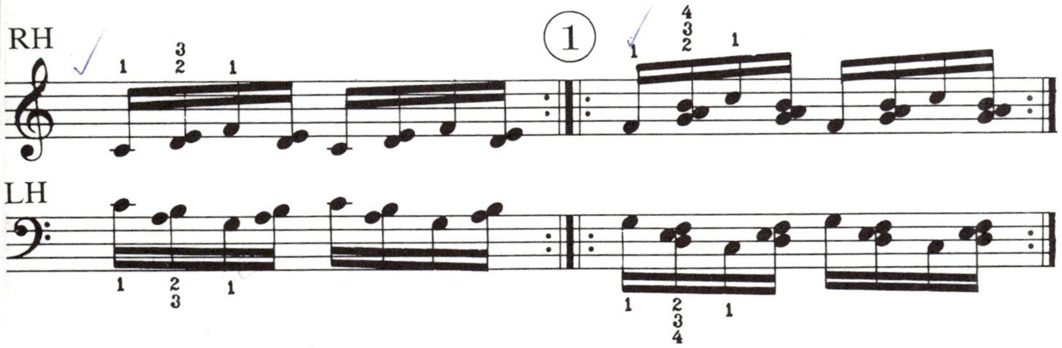

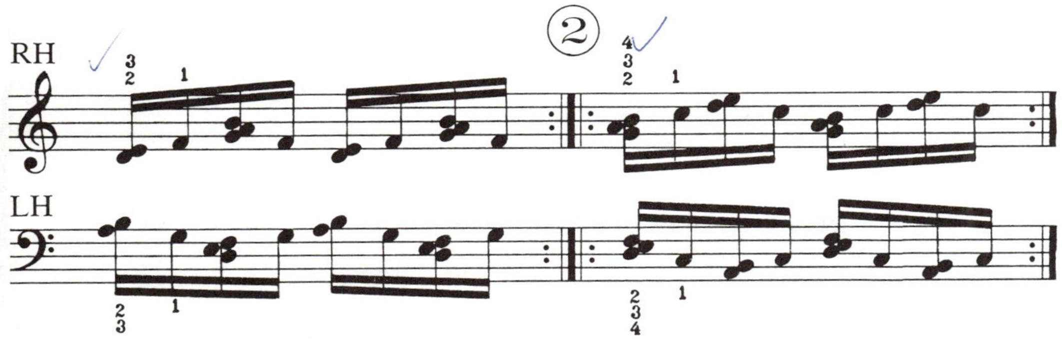

Repeat several times

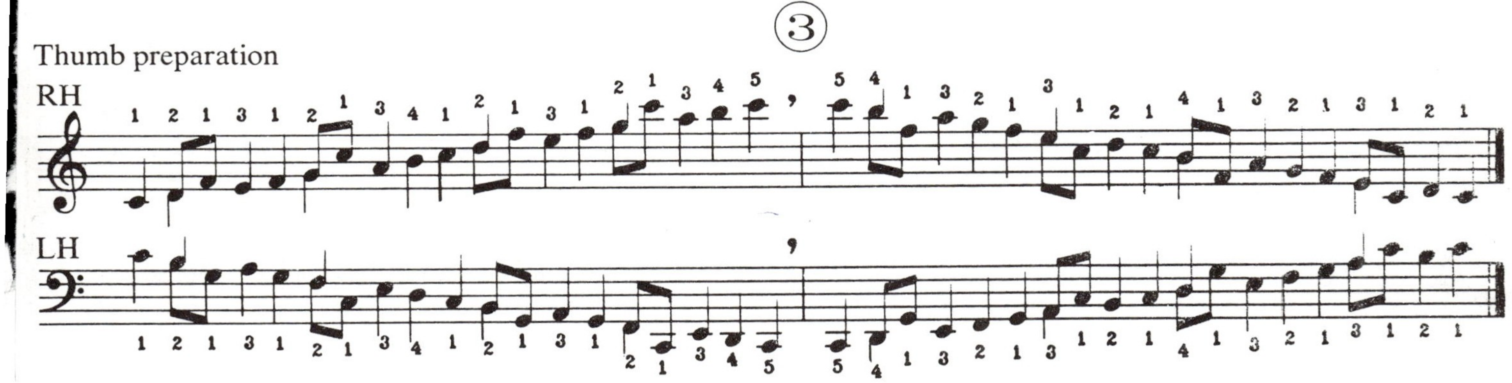

CHORD EXERCISES

These exercises should be learned in all positions and practiced hands separately as well as hands together in the required keys. These examples are in C major.

C. Poole

Repeat each exercise several times.

ADDITIONAL EAR TEST EXERCISES

1. Clap every rhythmic pattern until able to do so from memory.

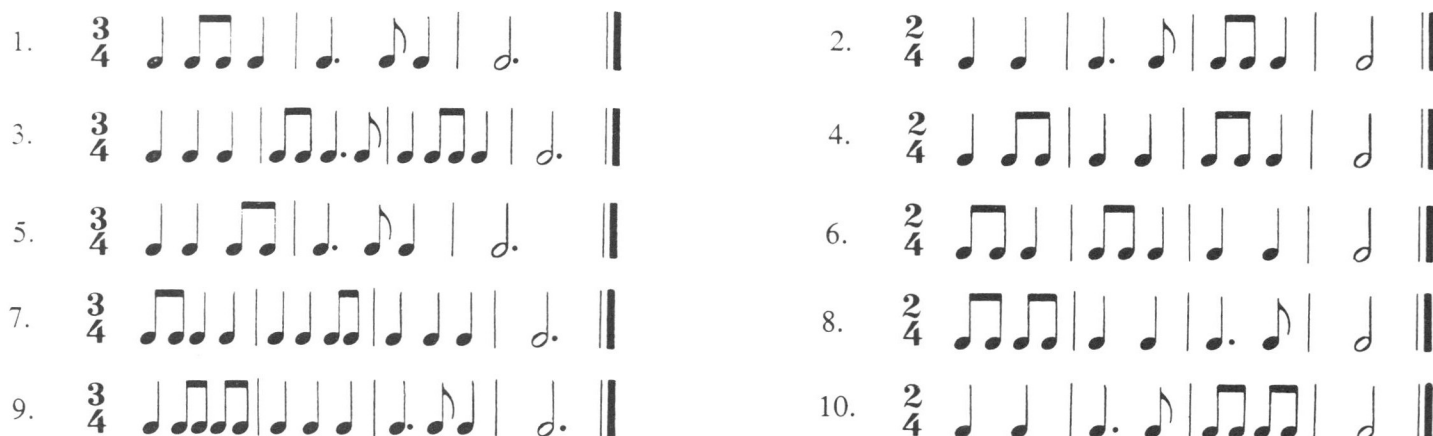

2. Complete the intervals.
Sound the interval on the piano, then sing both notes of the interval.

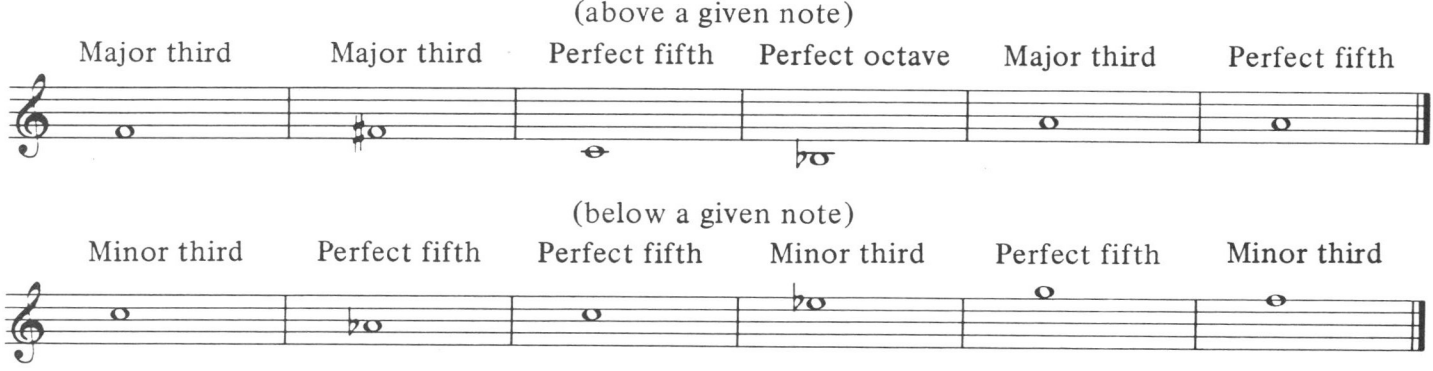

3. Using only the notes of the triad, invent a tune using the given rhythm. Then play the triad and sing the tune. Test by playing. (Dotted notes and half notes may be used.)